TEN HOUSES

TEN HOUSES

Edited by Oscar Riera Ojeda

Peter Forbes & Associates

2

ROCKPORT
PUBLISHERS

Rockport Publishers, Inc.
Gloucester, Massachusetts

First published in the United States of America by:

Rockport Publishers, Inc.

33 Commercial Street

Gloucester, Massachusetts 01930

Telephone: 508-282-9590

Fax: 508-283-2742

Other distribution by:

Rockport Publishers, Inc.

Gloucester, Massachusetts 01930

ISBN 1-56496-183-4

10 9 8 7 6 5 4 3 2 1

Cover Photo: House in Surry/Photo by Nick Wheeler Photography

Printed in Hong Kong by Midas Printing Limited

Graphic Design: Lucas H. Guerra / Oscar Riera Ojeda

Contents

Foreword

by Oscar Riera Ojeda

My first approximation to the work of Peter Forbes took place a few months after I had changed my residence, from the distant and humid Argentinean pampas, to the picturesque but climatically rigorous reality of New England.

Although based largely on my instinct and intuition, I began from that moment to acquire a high degree of respect and interest in his architecture, certain that the validity of his guiding principles would withstand a posterior and more meticulous analysis of his vertebral pieces.

After several journeys across the region, and an uninterrupted contact with this architect, time served only to reinforce my initial impression. During that period I was able to discover various aspects of his life that have had an unfailingly powerful impact upon his work.

Of all of these, perhaps the most significant among them is marked by his incredible knowledge and love for the land upon which the majority of his houses are implanted. This great affinity has allowed him to understand the limits to which he may venture (given the natural inclemencies that assault the perdurability of his buildings) in his avid interest to carry out constructive and technological innovations in every one of his works. This vast sophistication, carried over many of his details of materialization, has been accomplished, however, without altering the ever-present minimalist spirit or the sacred atmosphere of serenity that reigns inside as well as outside his buildings.

The respect for local traditions, both in their formal or linguistic aspects, as well as in their constructive realization, is another interesting theme in the work of Peter Forbes. And even when some of his houses display greater concessions in this sense, the final results have clearly reflected his irreproachable modernist essence.

This great capacity to respond to a place is what has assured that these ten houses attain the difficult and ambiguous objective of blending in mimetically with the landscape while, at the same time, enhancing it.

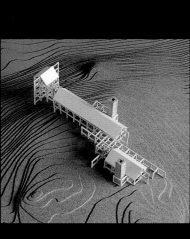

House at Cape Rosier

se at Seal Cove

House in Mattapoisett

House in Deer Isle

se on Great Cranberry Island

House in Marion

House on Potomac River

Introduction

by Pilar Viladas

Peter Forbes once told a journalist that in architecture, there is "a narrow [line] between Spartan and mean." The same could be said for the rugged New England landscape that has been the context for so many of the houses that Forbes has designed. Set mostly along the rocky, forested coasts of Maine an[d] Massachusetts, Forbes's houses are as spare and uncompromising as their sur-roundings, while they also capture the plain and elegant beauty of those settin[g]

New England looms large in Forbes's aesthetic and personal universe. He ha[s] spent most of his summers in a rambling, unelectrified, 1896 Shingle-style house on an island off the coast of Maine. It was here, as an avid sailor, that Forbes learned both the joys and the harsh realities of North Atlantic weath[er] and an appreciation for the functional elegance of shipbuilding—all of whic[h] inform his rigorous, yet sensual approach to architecture. He believes that a house, like a ship, must be designed without excess, to work and work well, but that it can—and indeed should—be beautiful, too.

It is no surprise that the shipbuilding analogy brings to mind Le Corbusier's hymn to steamships in *Vers Une Architecture*, in which he exhorts architects "prefer respect for the forces of nature to a lazy respect for tradition. . . [and]the majesty of solutions which spring from a problem that has been cle[ar]ly stated." Educated as a Modernist, Forbes knew and greatly admired Mies [van] der Rohe, and studied with Louis Kahn at Yale. He prefers strong, clear, abst[ract] forms to any direct historical quotation, although his abstraction is far from arbitrarily applied: Forbes's work displays a keen awareness of the peculiarit[ies] of site and context. His palette of materials is clearly Modernist—wood, stee[l,] stone, glass, and concrete—but even as he balances them with a cool restrai[nt,] the effect is always warm. Guiding Forbes's formal and material decisions ar[e a] graceful sense of proportion and an eagle-eyed attention to detail, both of which, given the architect's minimalist propensities, insure that his houses ar[e] often Spartan, but never mean.

Unlike many architects, Forbes is fortunate to have built most of his houses [on]

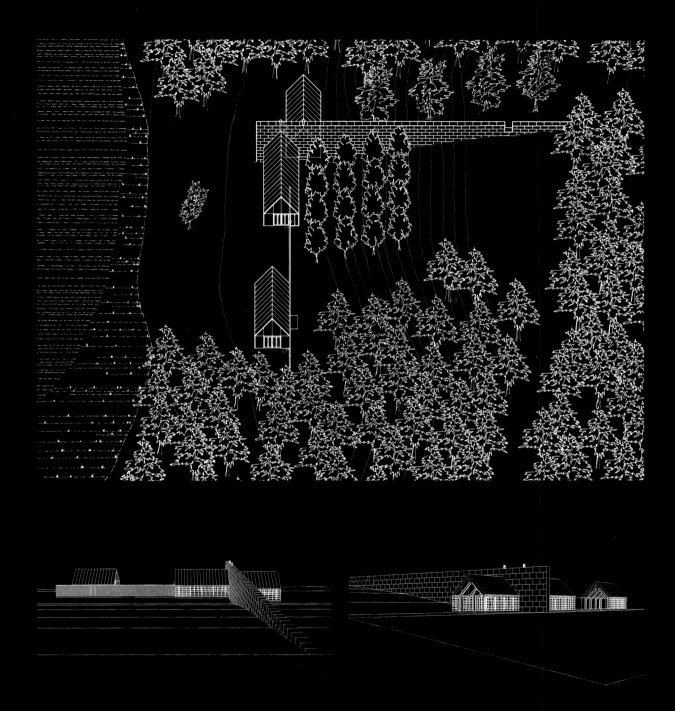

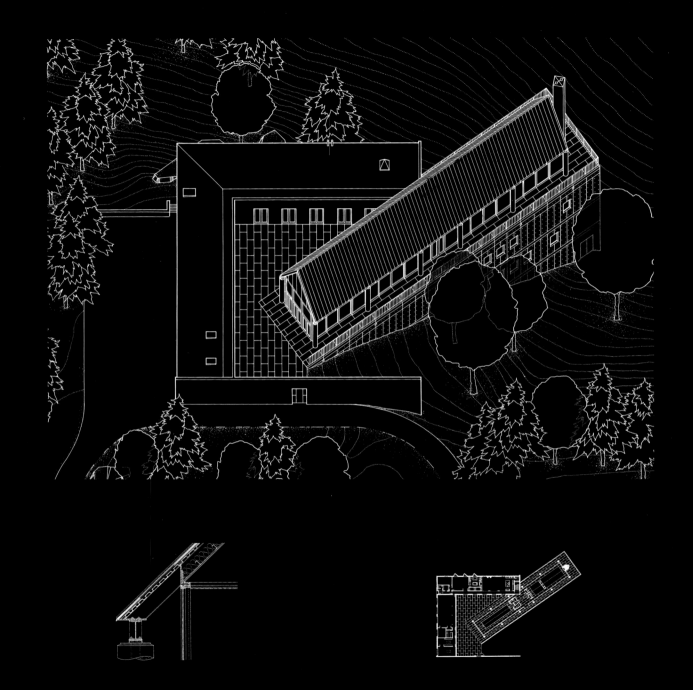

poised between deep forest and rocky seashore, and are therefore doubly blessed—a fact that is never lost on their designer. Forbes's response to these sites is invariably to create houses that take maximum advantage of their views while making a minimal impact on the site; they can be small and tall, as in the house at Seal Cove on Maine's Mount Desert Island, or long and narrow.

A number of the latter type are broken into a series of small, pavilion-like pieces, both to afford the various parts of the house optimum light and views, as well as to respect the contours of the site. The house Forbes designed on Great Cranberry Island, near Bar Harbor, Maine, and a house in Surry, Maine are examples of such an approach. In both houses, Forbes made the pavilions as open as possible, although by different means. The Cranberry Island house is a series of transverse bearing walls that allow the buildings' long walls to be made entirely of glass on both sides. In the house in Surry, a system of concrete structural columns supports the roof and allows the interiors of the pavilions to be open, unobstructed spaces. In both cases, the architecture doesn't so much occupy the landscape as frame it.

In all Forbes's houses, the New England vernacular of pitched roofs, clapboard and shingle walls, and stone chimneys is interpreted through an abstracted formal vocabulary that gives his buildings an almost archetypal quality. "Almost," because there is nothing archetypal about the sophisticated way in which the buildings are made. A simple gabled box and massive stone chimney become Minimalist sculpture by the time Forbes gets through with them, and they meet with a jeweler's precision. Even when he quotes architectural history most overtly, as in the houses he designed in Marion and Mattapoisett, Massachusetts, Forbes's sensibility is at heart Modernist. For example, the traditionally shingled and gabled exterior of the house in Mattapoisett encloses open, pared-down interiors; instead of timber beams, stainless steel cables brace the structure.

Not all Forbes's essays in domestic architecture are written on a backdrop of unspoiled nature. In a populous suburban neighborhood of Washington, D.C., the architect transformed what had been a modest 1950s house by running a

two-story, gabled shed right through it, and then covering the long walls and roof of the new structure in lead-coated copper—a move that makes the house appear both austere and grittily urban next to its politely pastichey neighbors. Only the glazed end walls of the house reveal the open, light-filled quality of its interior.

Still, it seems clear that Forbes will always be known—probably not as a household name, but rather to a small, select group of highly sophisticated, idiosyncratic, and independent-minded clients—for those uncompromising houses that dot the Maine coast and its islands. Forbes continues to explore the possibilities of the type in houses, like the one with the striking steel-tube structure, which he designed for a very forward-thinking grandmother, or the house he recently completed in Orcutt Harbor. A long, narrow extrusion of a house, it begins as a traditional shingled and gabled form but gradually dissolves, as it progresses toward the shoreline, into a porch of glass, wire, and open rafters. Along the way, the house bows slightly, in a conceptual nod to the "force field" of the owner's nearby radio tower. But this Modernist gesture can also be read in elevation as a historicist one: the bowed wall recalls its Shingle Style antecedents. Yet it does so in Forbes's typically understated manner. Like so many laconic, dignified Downeasters, Forbes's houses stand as a collective tribute to the virtues of choosing one's words carefully.

Previous Spread: Axonometric view and perspectives of House on Mill Island, a vacation home in Maine designed by Peter Forbes & Associates in 1986.
Left: Axonometric view, construction detail and floor plan of House in Boston, designed by Peter Forbes & Associates in 1986.

House at Seal Cove

Seal Cove, Maine

The house is a structurally simple building organized around a strong central axis oriented to the ocean. As one proceeds along this axis from the land to the sea, the building becomes progressively more transparent—windows in horizontal bands are more frequent, larger, and more closely spaced, accelerating toward the view. The axis culminates in a two-story triangular bay window commanding a 180-degree view of the cove and Blue Hill Bay.

The entrance level of the house is an entirely self-sufficient dwelling for the owners, the upper floor accommodates summer visitors, and a lower level, opening directly to the shore, provides a workshop, and repair.

Built under severe budget constraints, the Spartan finish is entirely compatible with the simple lines and strong geometry of the form. The spaces within are generous, and the framing, purposely left exposed, is of first class craftsmanship.

Above: The color, as well as the form of the house evolved from the environmental palette of dark rock ledges and sharply pointed fir trees; the house appearing to grow out of the landscape, a bold form, but one in harmony with nature.

Opposite Page: The strong vertical of the two story bay window and the steep roof give a much greater presence than the small area of the house would otherwise suggest. The proportions of the building are in sympathy with the scale of the landscape, commanding the cove and the ocean beyond.

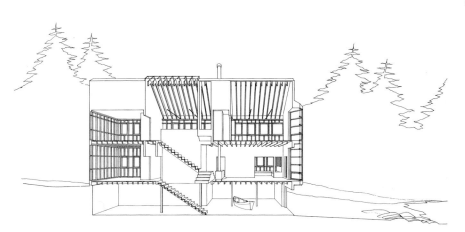

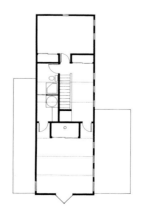

Second Floor Plan

0   10 feet

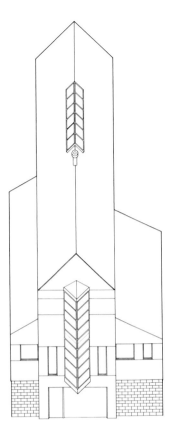

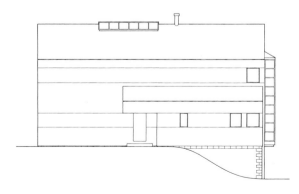

This Page: *The axial force of the house is reinforced by the repetitive sequence of the structural elements: exposed wall and roof framing, tie rods and ridge beam. The spaces follow the structure with rooms, stairs, and their relationship to the outdoors articulated by the expressed construction of the building.*

Opposite Page: *The unadorned elemental form of the house, immediately apparent as it is approached form the land side, is reminiscent of the barns and utilitarian structures of Maine, but reduced and abstracted to a sculptural icon.*

House in Mattapoisett

Mattapoisett, Massachusetts

S ited on a sandy island only fourteen feet above the high-tide line, the program presented a series of conflicting design imperatives: a spectacular view of Buzzards Bay and the Elizabeth Islands, but severe exposure from the identical quarter; an advantageous wintertime southern frontage, but little protection from the ceaseless southwest summer wind. The need for a year-round dwelling that also accommodates summer visitors posed contradictions of intimacy and scale.

The resolution is a house that opens to the outdoors with a facade of 100 feet of triple-hung windows allowing continuous access to the deck and beach beyond. In front of the window wall a separate steel structure supports wooden shutters, ten feet square, which, when open, form sun and summer wind screens and, when closed, present a strong defense to seasonal storms. The building itself is laterally braced by shear walls and diagonal stainless-steel cables that connect to an unbroken rear wall to establish a strong, resilient structural system. The traditional building materials and forms of the area—cedar shingles and simple geometric forms—are pared down to their simplest representation, devoid of any trim or decoration, to emphasize the abstract manifestation of "house."

Above Right: The entrance, sharply carved through the tower that connects the main wing with the guest wing, offers a carefully framed view of lawn, cedar trees, and the ocean beyond. It is a gate to the private realm of the house.

Opposite page: The front of the house facing a public road and the harsh northern exposure is closed, largely windowless, forming a protective enclosure against intrusion and the winter winds.

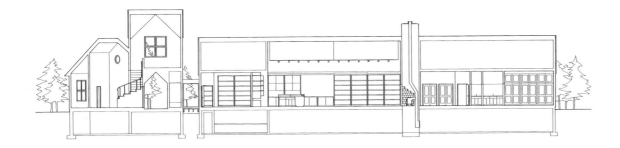

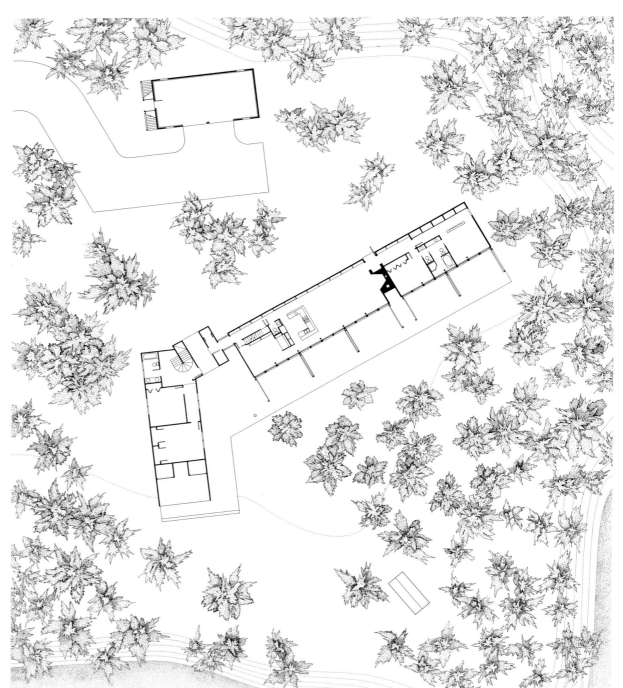

Left: *Within the enclosing wings of the house the building unfolds in a composition of triple-hung windows, storm shutters, and decks; still prepared to resist the force of the natural elements, but offering a gracious space for family outdoor living and entertaining guests.*

Opposite Page: *The long, simple ridge line, broken only by the entrance tower and the chimney, resonates with the powerful horizon of the adjacent beaches, sandbars, and the open ocean beyond.*

Above Right: *The triple-hung windows provide unobstructed access to the continuous decks from every room of the house, a particular requirement of the owners, and allow ample ventilation in the warm, humid summers.*

Right: *To protect the house from ocean storms—this site is the exact point where most hurricanes strike the New England coast—ten-foot square shutters constructed of wood reinforced with steel can be closed over the continuous wall of triple-hung windows.*

Above: *During the winter, the low sun penetrates through the south-facing window wall to provide substantial solar heat, which augments the deep-well geo-thermal heating system of the house. In the summer the windows are shaded by the slightly over-hanging roof and the shadows of oak and cedar trees.*

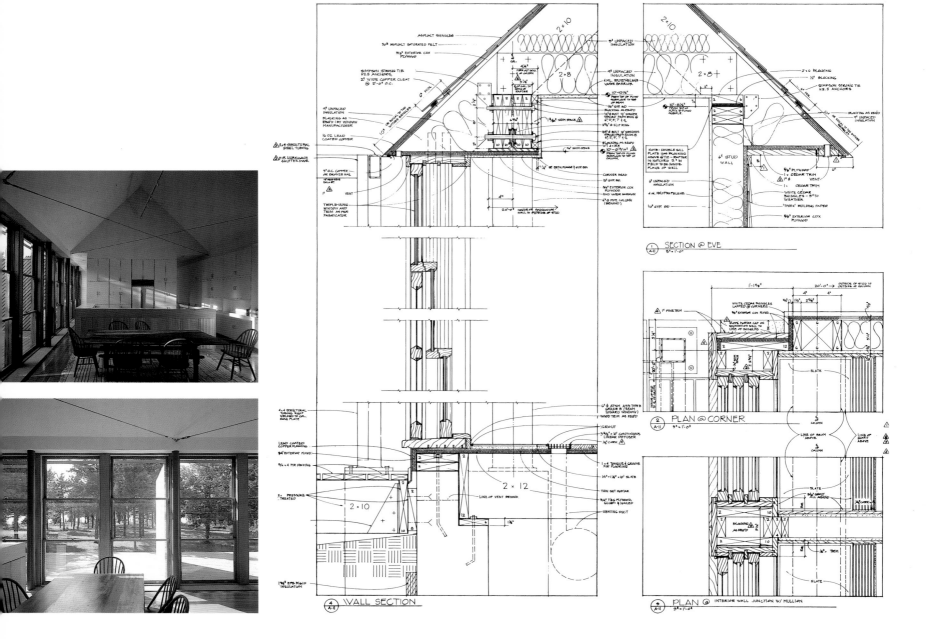

Left: The Great Room serves as living, dining, and kitchen space, and reflects the exterior form of the house in the interiors. The room is focused on an unusual "fireplace," a niche constructed of brick and stone, within which is an iron wood-burning stove. The niche serves to absorb and then radiate the heat of the stove, while protecting the surrounding plaster walls.

Opposite Page: The open storm shutters, perpendicular to the window wall, form exterior rooms, open to the sun and air, but gently protected from the strong afternoon ocean breezes.

House on Deer Isle

Deer Isle, Maine

The extraordinary, but fragile beauty of an ocean-side site led to a design that carefully juxtaposes the constructed object with the natural environment. Uncompromisingly man-made in both its geometry and materials —glass, leaded copper, and cut stone—the house reflects or dissolves into the landscape without compromising its own formal integrity.

The house is composed of two pavilions: master bedroom, and living/dining/kitchen. Each is defined by concrete piers at the corners, which support tubular steel trusses spanning the entire space to carry the laminated cedar roof deck. Exterior walls, free of any load-bearing function, are glass. Massive stone chimneys stand nearly free of the pavilions, visually anchoring the composition to the surrounding ledges.

The program required several subordinate houses for various family members and their guests. Together, these constitute a family of buildings attendant to the glass house, which serves as the parent's dwelling and principal gathering place for meals and social activities. By its siting, the cluster of pavilions directs physical and visual exploration of the site and forms an inner space among the buildings that is manicured, polished, and serene. Beyond the perimeter of this civilized clearing, nature immediately prevails—birch and spruce forest, rocky promontory, and the ocean itself.

Above: *Seen from the sea shore, the house appears to grow out of the rock ledges that form the site. The chimneys are built of native stone, blending into the landscape. The attached pavilions become transparent tents, ephemeral structures reflecting every change in season or weather.*

Opposite Page: *The transparent pavilions form a screen to the magnificent view, controlling the observer's experience in a series of glimpses between columns, trees or chimneys until the moment when each vista is revealed, each enhanced by the sense of anticipation developed by the experience.*

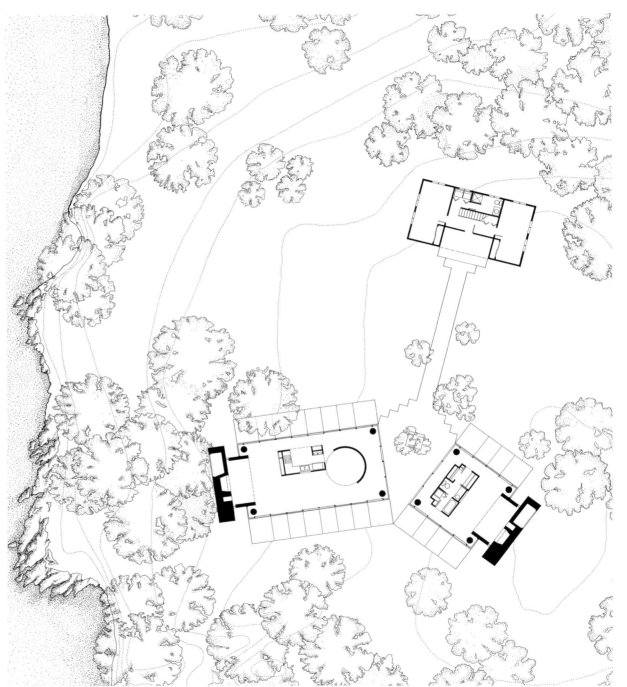

Left: *The most powerful spatial moment in the composition of the three pavilions is the wedge of space between the two glass buildings, as if the air were made more dense by the pressure of the two glass walls being forced apart and the presence of the third pavilion at the end of its stone path. This is the point from which the view of the ocean is ultimately revealed.*

Opposite Page: *The glass pavilions are opened to one another, exchanging reflections and a continuity of space.*

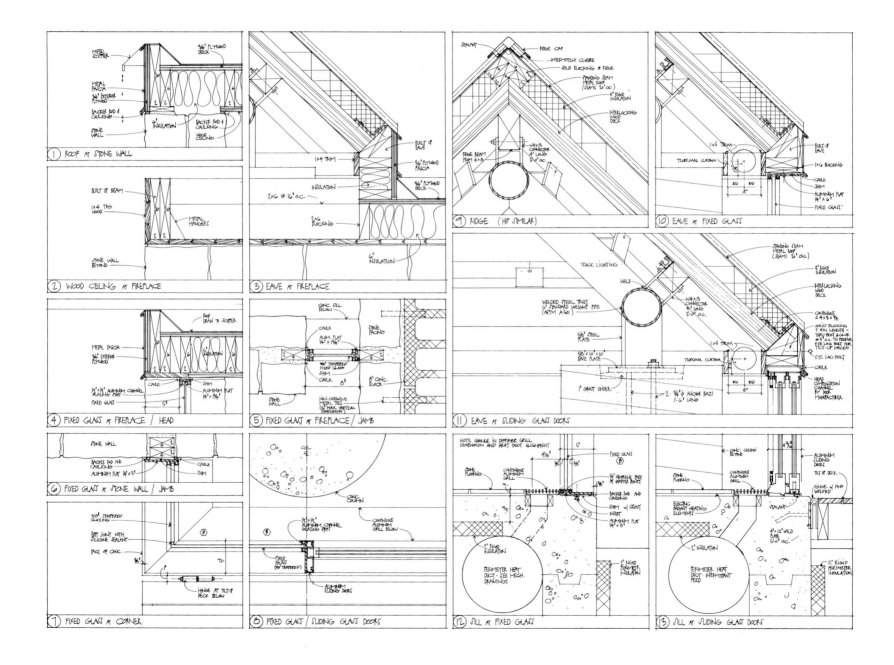

Above Left: *Where the chimneys penetrate under the pavilion roofs, a deep inglenook is formed, a separate room for the fireplace or, as if the fireplace had become an inhabitable space.*

Left: *Under the tent-like roof structure of steel tubes and cedar planking are separate enclosures for the dining area and the kitchen. The dining area is contained within a curved screen of gray cedar. The kitchen inhabits a separate "house," complete with a window that aligns with a distant island and light house.*

Right: Although both of the principal pavilions are essentially a single room, both achieve a great deal of spatial complexity and excitement from the juxtaposition of the subforms within the rooms.

Opposite Page: The chimneys penetrate to form strong hearth enclosures, the separate "houses" of the kitchen and bathroom describe a sequence of entry, passage, and arrival spaces by their relationship to the exterior glass partition.

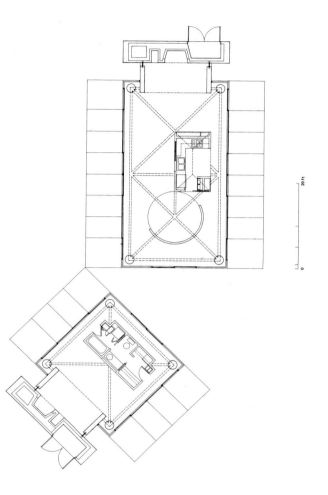

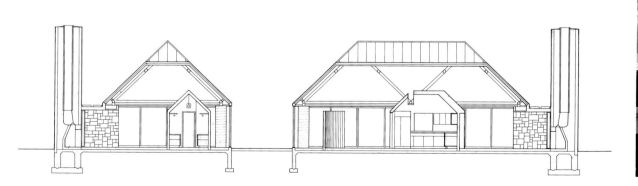

House on Great Cranberry Island

Great Cranberry Island, Maine

Two long, glass-walled pavilions are drawn across this coastal site at the juncture of dense forest and open meadow to strengthen and articulate the natural division of the landscape. At a break between the pavilions, two massive stone chimneys form a gateway, allowing passage from the lush woods to the barren ocean frontage and directing entry into the house.

Divided into family accommodations and guest quarters, the spaces are intentionally very simple in their organization and geometric form in order to frame and set off the remarkable natural setting—on one side, the immediate miniature landscape of rocks and mosses on the forest floor, while on the other the sheer dramatic landscape of sparse grass, black basalt ledges, and the open sea.

Structurally and formally the building is a series of transverse-bearing walls carrying the roof deck. The walls are pierced by large and small openings to provide a continuous sequence of varied spaces. Free of any load-bearing function, the exterior longitudinal walls are entirely sliding glass panels framed in teak and mahogany. All of the interior and exterior surfaces are otherwise of wood—cedar, mahogany, or douglas fir.

Above: *Seen from the shore across its open meadow, the house hugs the ground, the roof ridge line below the trees, the entire composition consciously subordinate to the natural condition of the site, but defining the transitions from open space to dense forest, meadow grass to pine woods.*

Opposite Page: *Beyond Great Cranberry Island there is no other land, no further islands only the open sea. The gateway formed by the stone chimneys directs and frames the view to the ocean, articulating even the distant horizon that would otherwise remain an indefinable expanse.*

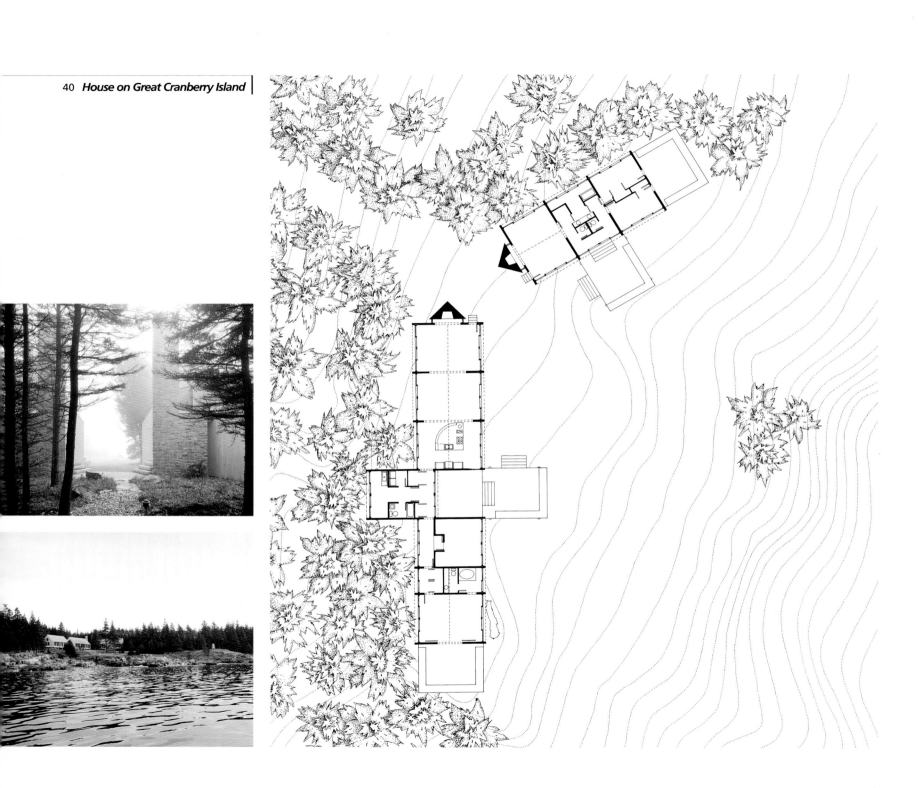

Left: *The two arms of the house align not with the edge of the sea shore, but, rather, with the rock ledges that run obliquely into the sea.*

Opposite Page: *Exposed to extreme ocean weather conditions and often shrouded in fog, the house had to be built to withstand both violent forces and the effects of nearly continuous moisture. Like a boat, the house is built of rot-resistant woods, such as cedar and teak, and lead for weather proofing. Even the chimneys act as stone "ballast," anchoring the wood structure against the force of the wind.*

Above: *One bay of the main house is pulled back into the woods to form a sheltered deck on the ocean side. Out of the wind, adjacent to the kitchen, this space is used by the owners for outside dining or reading.*

Opposite Page: *From a distance the house is quite integral with the site. However, at more immediate range it can be seen that the long pavilions hover over the contours of the land on concrete piers.*

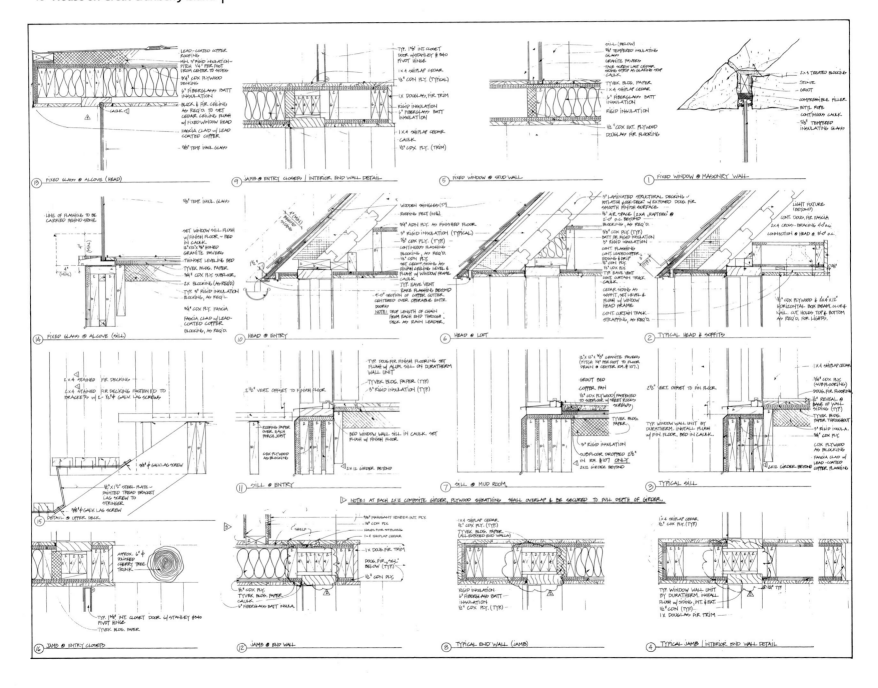

13 FIXED GLASS @ ALCOVE (HEAD)

9 JAMB @ ENTRY CLOSETS / INTERIOR END WALL DETAIL

5 FIXED WINDOW @ STUD WALL

1 FIXED WINDOW @ MASONRY WALL

14 FIXED GLASS @ ALCOVE (SILL)

10 HEAD @ ENTRY

6 HEAD @ LOFT

2 TYPICAL HEAD & SOFFITS

15 DETAIL @ UPPER DECK

11 SILL @ ENTRY

7 SILL @ MUD ROOM

3 TYPICAL SILL

NOTE: AT EACH 2X12 COMPOSITE GIRDER, PLYWOOD SHEATHING SHALL OVERLAP & BE SECURED TO FULL DEPTH OF GIRDER.

16 JAMB @ ENTRY CLOSETS

12 JAMB @ END WALL

8 TYPICAL END WALL (JAMB)

4 TYPICAL JAMB / INTERIOR END WALL DETAIL

Above Left: *The kitchen, dining room, and living room are each defined by the bearing walls that span the house every sixteen feet. However, the "telescope" effect of each opening getting progressively wider from the chimney to the kitchen connects the spaces by reversing the effects of perspective.*

Left: *An order of materials articulates the structural concept of the house. All structural walls are clad in cedar. All non-structural walls are of mahogany. All spanning materials—roof and floors—are of Douglas fir.*

House in Marion

Marion, Massachusetts

Sited in a commanding position on the brow of a hill forested with tall pines, this house, by its location, formal geometry, and symmetry establishes a presence far stronger than its modest size would seem to allow. The form builds up from the hillside to apsidal porches at each end, to tall chimneys and steep roofs, culminating in the central tower with its contemporary interpretation of a "widow's walk."

Integral to the design was the owner's involvement with competitive sailing and the requirements that this interest engendered. The house is sited to allow an expansive view of the Buzzards Bay racing area, and the tower, porches, and angles provide the client with ideal places for observation of weather and wind conditions. From a trap door in the floor of the "widow's walk," sails can be hoisted inside the tower to dry for the next day's racing. The two- and one-half-story space soars through the house; the central stair laces back and forth through it, tying the entire composition of spaces together. This central space is at its best on summer mornings, with the first light breeze rustling the brilliant dacron of a drying spinnaker, gently pervading the rest of the house with sound and color, and a sense of anticipation.

Above: *The verandah penetrates the tower, both internally and externally, breaking down the distinction between interior and exterior space and facilitating circulation, an important consideration for the owners' use of the house for entertaining groups of people.*

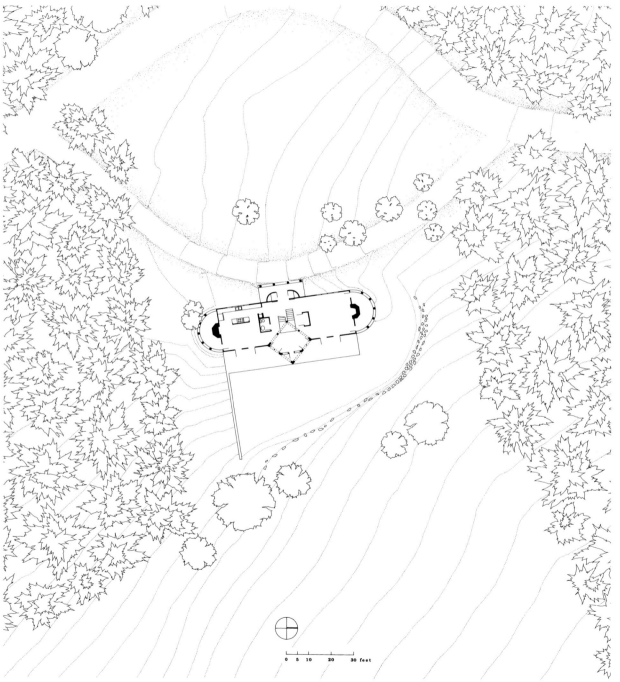

0 5 10   20   30 feet

Above Left: *The entry, on the land side of the house, is formed by a curved vestibule and coat room within the cover of the roof over-hang. Like all the porches, the entry is constructed of concrete columns, which extend from the foundation to the eaves.*

Left: *Seen from the ends, the house is a narrow but complex form, building up in a sequence of elements. The composition is designed to make the transition from longitudinal to transverse, as the house shifts from being a wall along a hillside to being a tower confronting the distant view.*

Right: In the winter, with the sailing exploits of the owners temporarily suspended, the house remains an active second home. With the leaves gone from the surrounding trees and the landscape abstracted by a blanket of snow, the topographic quality of the house becomes much more apparent. The complex roof forms and the pyramidal composition of the house tie it directly to the form of the site.

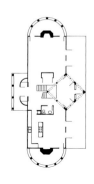

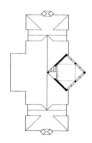
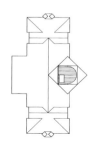

Above: *Across the great meadow, the apparent scale of the house is much larger than its actual modest size. The careful manipulation of the roof forms, the exploitation of the plastic quality of shingles, and the articulation of the geometry, in order to cast strong shadows, all serve to relate a small house to its large context.*

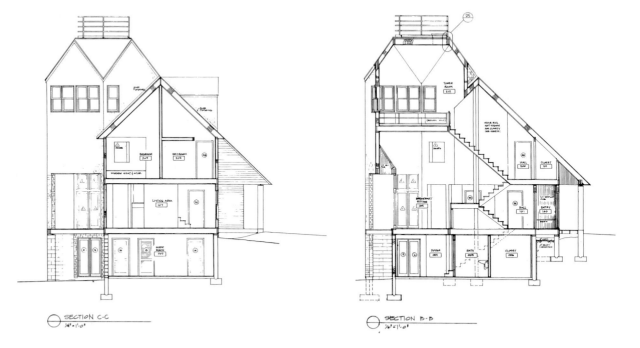

SECTION C-C
1/4" = 1'-0"

SECTION B-B
1/4" = 1'-0"

SECTION A-A
1/4" = 1'-0"

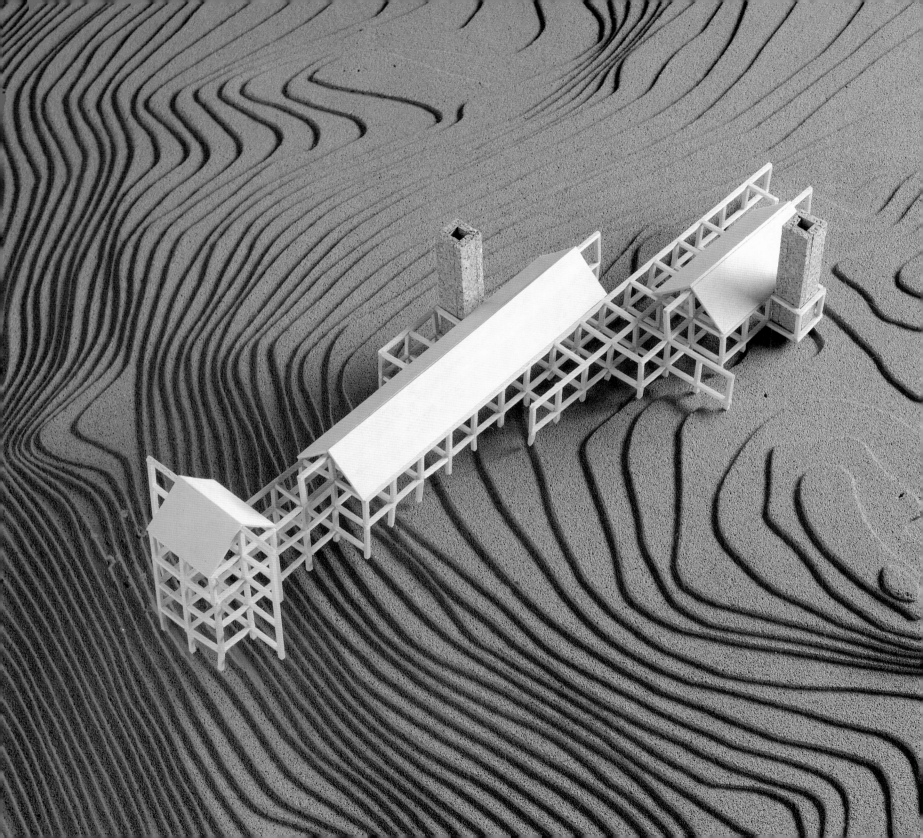

House at Cape Rosier

Cape Rosier, Maine

T he site, a promontory jutting into Penobscot Bay, is a landscape of open spruce woods and granite outcrop-
pings with very little forest-floor vegetation. The immediate view is of the forest, with the ocean frontage
obscured by steep cliffs. The distant view is a perspective of islands and open sea. Within this transparent landscape the house is a transparent composition of structure with minimal enclosure.

The structure and formal order of the building is established by a three-dimensional grid of eight-inch-square timbers
forming eight-foot cubes of space. Cast across the site, the grid forms three dwelling areas—main house, guest house,
and study—as if the intensity of use was reflected in the density of the enclosure. Surrounding porches, pergolas, and
bridges are proportionately less dense, with the grid fading off into the woods as free-standing posts and lintels, blurring
the distinction between the transparent construction and the transparent forest.

Within the three enclosures the spatial definition is equally minimalist. Kitchen, bathrooms, and closets are treated as
free-standing furniture, and furniture itself is kept to a minimum. Only at the two hearths, the focus of the dwellings,
does the space become so dense as to coalesce into prisms of stone.

Above: Access to the house is a path that
wraps around a prominent knoll to arrive at the
off-set of guest and main pavilions. Drawn by
glimpses of the ocean through dense woods,
the explorer navigates through internal sub-
structures and the grid itself to discover the
trestle to the study and the ultimate resolution
of the experience in a view of a distant island.

Opposite Page: The enclosed living space,
defined by the simple roof forms, shift in
response to the landscape, view, and sequence
of spatial exploration.

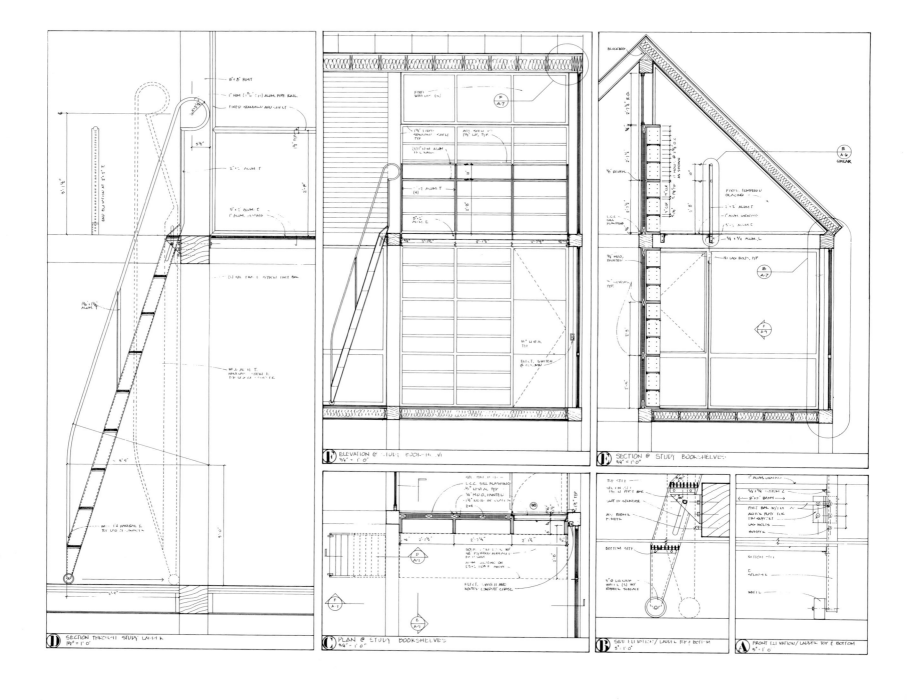

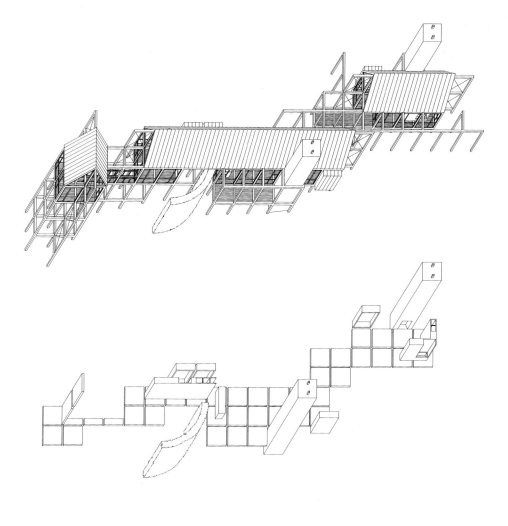

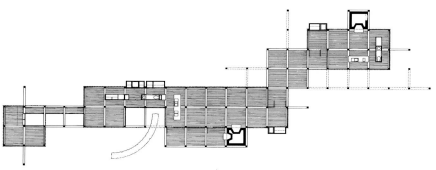

Left: *The construction of the house is clearly articulated as a "kit of parts." The structural frame of timber posts and beams is assembled with hidden fasteners. All of the construction fits as replicable components: floor panels within which are packaged all the utilities, walls of either glass in thin steel frames or pre-fabricated storage modules of plywood and cedar.*

Opposite Page: *In the study, bookshelves extend up to the ridge and are accessible via a light steel mezzanine system clipped to the timber frame.*

House on Potomac River

Washington, D.C.

I n an archetypical suburban setting, this house sits in a row of detached single-family houses, all built in the early 1950s, all with nearly identical floor plans, each sited twelve feet from the next along a genuinely beautiful street that overlooks the Potomac River.

Strictly aligned with their property lines, the existing houses face slightly, disturbingly, away from the view. Built through the "ruins" of one of the typical houses, this building corrects the alignment by skewing perpendicular to the river, while incorporating the footprint of the original house with its orderly relationship to the rest of the neighborhood. The vestiges of the original brick walls remain as an entry and kitchen with adjacent courtyards, and continue through the new building as the dining room/stairwell wall.

The new structure is light wood frame with both roof and exterior walls sheathed in lead-coated copper, not dissimilar from many traditional tin-clad Southern buildings. The plan organization itself follows that model—an open-breezeway house oriented to the prevailing summer wind as well as the view. Largely closed to the adjacent neighbors, the house maintains everyone's privacy and acknowledges the scale and pattern of its surroundings.

Above: The simple pewter-colored lead-coated copper walls make a pleasing foil for the patterns of shade and flowering trees that are the most important defining element of the neighborhood.

Opposite Page: Within the context of the suburban neighborhood, the house consciously follows the precedent of simple forms and small scale, while breaking with that tradition to more accurately reflect the realities of neighborliness in a congested living situation.

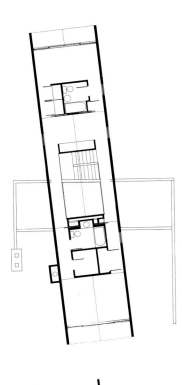

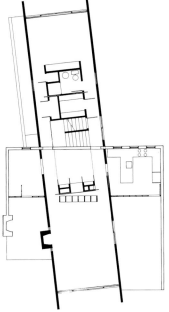

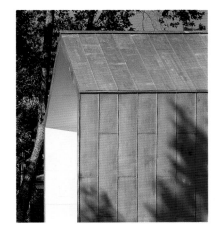

Top: *The exterior jacket of the house extends beyond the line of enclosure at each end to shield the living space from the noise of overhead aircraft traffic.*

Center: *The entrance occupies space between the existing "ruin" and the new construction.*

Bottom: *The rear of the house takes advantage of grade change to provide windows to a lower-level apartment.*

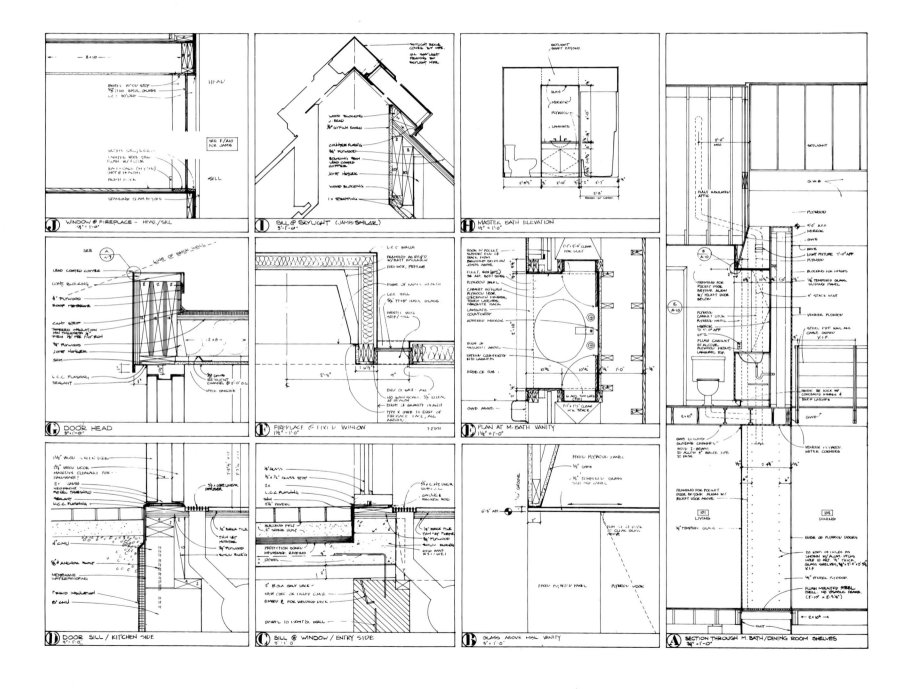

Left: *Elevated a full story above the street on a landscaped knoll, the transparent house loses little privacy to the immediate passer-by. Only from the park along the river (and with the prying lens of the architectural photographer) is the true extent of the transparency revealed. From the street, the house remains in the dusk a glowing enigmatic jewel box.*

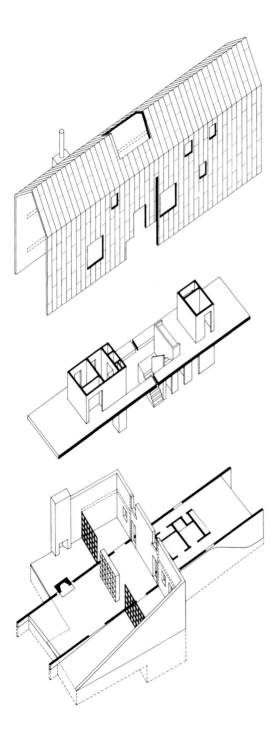

Left: *At the intersection of the two spatial volumes—that formed by the low pre-existing structure and the lofty nave of the new—the space rises unobstructed to the roof and a translucent insulated skylight.*

Opposite Page: *Looking from the entry through the intersection of the new building to the kitchen beyond, the layering of space is articulated by both the materials of each sequential surface and by the different qualities of light in each space.*

House on Mount Desert Island

Mount Desert Island, Maine

Three important concerns of the owner combined to generate the formal order of this house. First, the landscape of the area, both immediate and distant, is essential to the owner's daily experience. Second, natural light and the passage of time—daily and seasonally—are important sources of pleasure to the owner. Third, the owner is acutely allergic to a myriad of substances, both natural and man-made, and cannot be exposed to them for prolonged periods of time.

The formal response to these concerns has been to create an open framework of steel tubes—open to avoid mold and dust accumulation, steel as an inert and non-allergenic material—within which floors and rooms are platforms floating in space. Inside the building the only partitions are to separate bathrooms and closets, and these are of cedar with a water-based stain finish. Since plywood, gypsum wallboard, plaster, and most paints are receptors of molds and generators of toxins, they could not be present in the dwelling. The exterior walls of the living spaces are entirely glass and aluminum.

The open, glass-enclosed space is suffused with light, constantly changing through the course of the day and the year. The steel frame casts its pattern and, in turn, receives the lattice of shadows cast by the window-wall. Similarly, the open, transparent structure dissolves into the landscape—platforms in the forest to observe and experience nature. Rising to forty feet in the trees, the house affords a spectacular view of both the immediate environment and the distant mountains of Acadia National Park.

Above: Rising in a clearing on the brow of a hill, the house gently commands its site without disturbing the natural surroundings. The land was disturbed as little as possible during construction and replanted with native blueberry and bunchberry sod. A grove of white birch trees has been planted on the same grid as the house structure to mediate the transition from man-made to natural environment.

Opposite Page: The elements of the house construction are of a scale in keeping with the trees, rocks, and landforms of the site. This scalar relationship is as important as the transparency of the house in establishing its intimacy with the landscape.

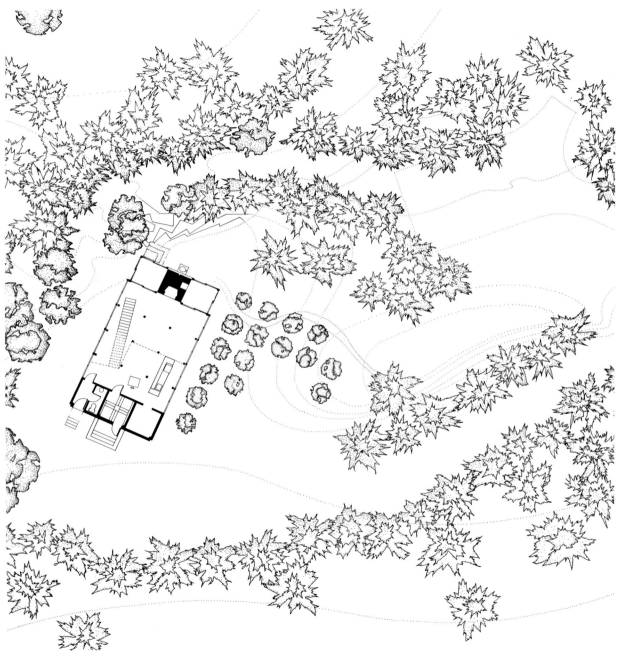

Left: *To effect the transition between land and structure, a set of monumental slabs of rough-cut native granite form the entrance steps. The stainless-steel roof scupper spills into a carved-stone catch-basin.*

Opposite Page: *One of the cubes of space defined by the house grid is occupied by the fireplace, a cube of concrete sculpted to also function as a massive scupper draining the steep metal roof.*

Right: *The intersection of the lofty interior living space with the low entry, porch, and hearth forms a transition zone of preparation for a change in environment, from inside to outside, a ceremonial event essential in a building where every other design gesture seeks to eliminate the separation of those two realms.*

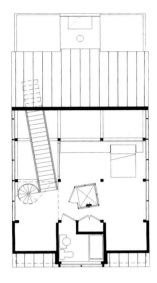

Second Level Plan

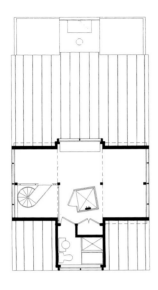

Dormer Plan

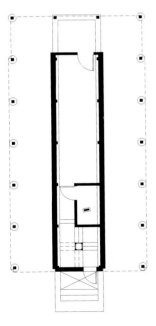

Foundation Plan

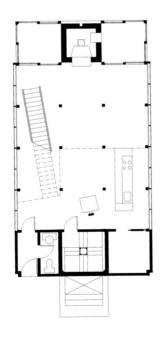

First Level Plan

This Page: At different times of day, and in different seasons, the house changes from an opaque object set in the landscape to an elusive mirror reflecting its surroundings to a transparent prism, camouflaged by nature itself.

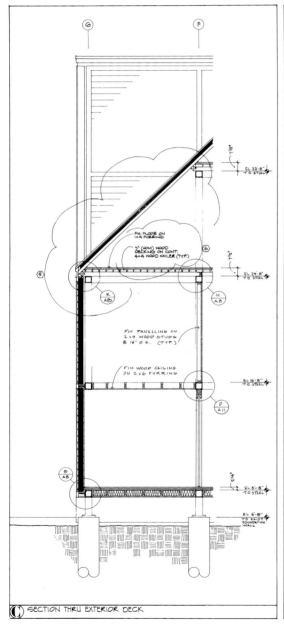

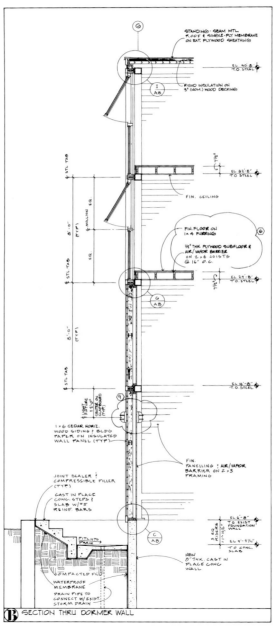

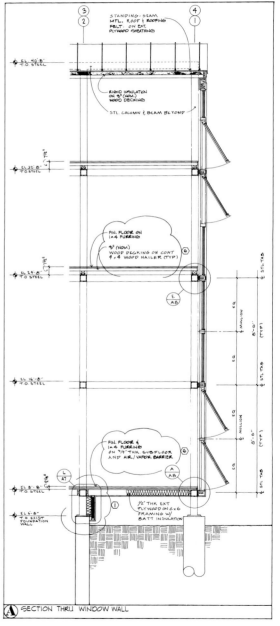

C SECTION THRU EXTERIOR DECK

B SECTION THRU DORMER WALL

A SECTION THRU WINDOW WALL

Right: Welded steel tubes satisfy the requirement for a structure that encloses space without interior walls, a requirement dictated by the multiple allergies of the owner and the need to circulate and exchange air without impediment. Within the steel grid, rooms can be platforms hanging in space, separated by space and geometry alone.

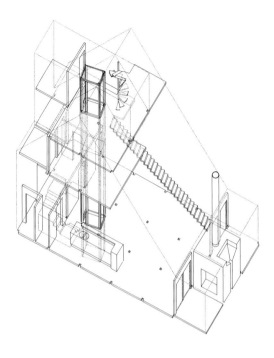

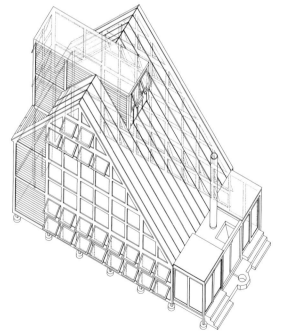

Top: *From the second-level platform, space flows over the cabinetry that forms a parapet, down through the grid cut by the stair, around the structure to join with the space below.*

Center: *On the second level the elevator is enclosed with finely perforated metal screen, which acts like a theater scrim.*

Bottom: *Leaping through the grid at an oblique angle, the main stair establishes a grid for circulation, which is followed by the orientation of the elevator beyond and the spiral stair above.*

This Page: *Although the entire living space is un-partitioned, the strong geometry of the grid defines different living areas within the larger envelope. There is a distinct sense of spatial differentiation in the cube of space by the fireplace, as opposed to the cube of space inhabited by the dining table, even though these two areas are immediately adjacent.*

Opposite Page: *Seen from the glass elevator rising through the open grid, disconnected from any floor, the prismatic quality of the house is most apparent.*

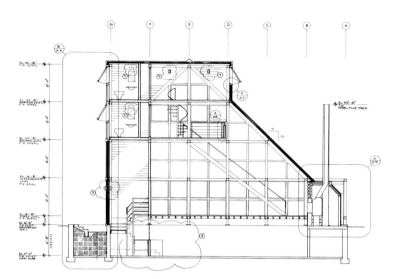

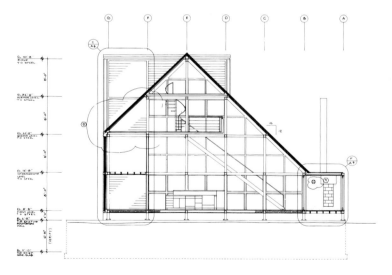

House at Orcutt Harbor

Orcutt Harbor, Maine

Three processions determine the order and form of this house. First, the building form processes across the site, starting at the point of access to the property and extending to the legal setback from the water's edge. The house acts as a formal bridge from the deep woods to the steep rocks of the shore, beginning as a protecting, closed form and gradually unfolding to take advantage of the views.

On a functional level, the house progresses from the enclosed utilitarian demands of garage, shop, and laundry to the private realms of bedrooms, to the open areas of public entertaining. As in the formal procession across the site, this programmatic procession is physically manifested in the gradual dissolution of enclosing walls into glass, the expansion of one's perception from the defined edges of a room to the limitless horizon.

In addition to these formal and functional transitions, there is an historical progression from the archetypal American house to the far more ephemeral, relativistic notion of dwelling in our present, less-structured society. The building begins as a highly traditional gable-end house, firmly anchored to its surroundings, but then it extrudes toward the horizon, accelerating in the frequency and size of its openings, shedding its dormers, enclosing walls and, ultimately, its roof. Finally, the form vibrates into thin air, a composition of pure glass, open rafters, and taut wires scarcely in contact with the ground below. The only hesitation in this accelerating procession is at the slight deformation where the linear form passes the implied force field of the owner's radio transmission tower. This temporary moment of deceleration, emphasized by a circular arrival platform, identifies the formal entrance and establishes a cross axis with the chimney and the hearth within.

Above: *Upon entering the site, the first view of the house is this gable end, highly evocative of traditional New England structures. Only the rigorous elimination of trim and detail reveal its modernist antecedents in addition to its traditional ones.*

Opposite Page: *Turning the corner of the house, its extraordinary length and the gradual dissolution of the form are exposed. As the building accelerates toward the shore, the spacing of solid elements—dormers, the chimney—become less frequent and then disappear completely. Conversely, openings in the fabric of the building—doors, windows, porches—occur more frequently and become larger until the wall and roof dissolve.*

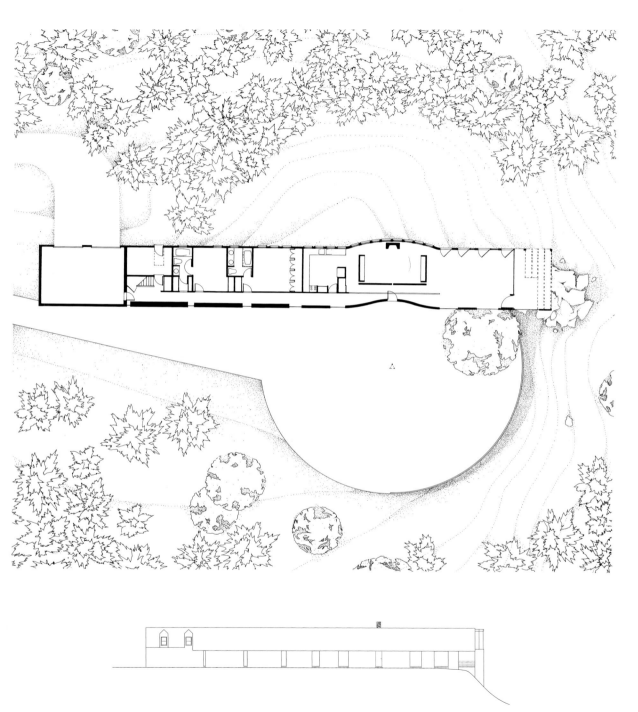

Left: At the ocean end of the house the roof enclosure dissolves, exposing the naked rafters, the walls reach their minimum thickness and glass is eliminated from the openings.

Opposite Page: On the north side of the house, severely minimal openings filled with fixed glazing proceed toward a horizon formed by the edge of a steep drop toward the ocean.

Right: *Opposite the inward curve at the front door, the house curves out on the south side, absorbing the fireplace and chimney within the building. The curve and the dissolution of the wall fabric is articulated by a gradual increase in the height of windows defining the bay.*

Opposite Page: *As the house reaches its seaward end it projects over the lip of a steep drop toward the shore and a retaining wall of massive granite blocks. The effect of this transition from firmly grounded wall to floating plane contributes to the expression of acceleration.*

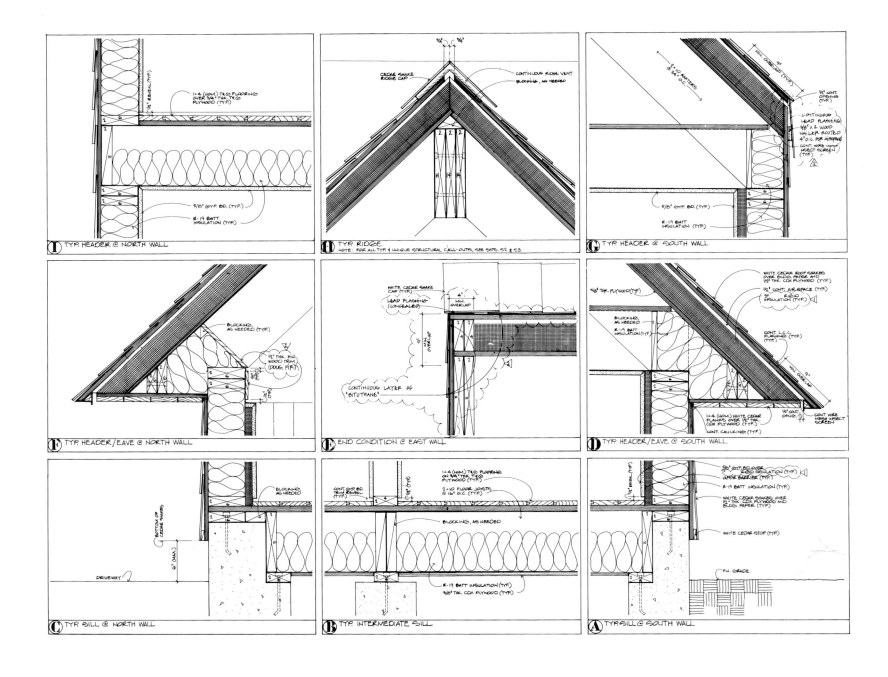

I. TYP. HEADER @ NORTH WALL

H. TYP. RIDGE
NOTE: FOR ALL TYP. & UNIQUE STRUCTURAL CALL-OUTS, SEE SHTS. S2 & S3

G. TYP. HEADER @ SOUTH WALL

F. TYP. HEADER/EAVE @ NORTH WALL

E. END CONDITION @ EAST WALL

D. TYP. HEADER/EAVE @ SOUTH WALL

C. TYP. SILL @ NORTH WALL

B. TYP. INTERMEDIATE SILL

A. TYP. SILL @ SOUTH WALL

Right: *Along the north side of the house a corridor connects the various private living spaces, ultimately opening into the more public living/dining room. The exterior wall of this corridor becomes progressively thinner at each window opening.*

Opposite Page: *To a height of eight feet the interior finish of the house is highly refined. Above the eight foot level, the muscular structure of the roof is revealed. The structure of Douglas fir rafters ripples and flexes to accommodate the sensuous curves of the building.*

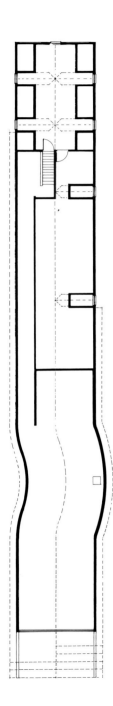
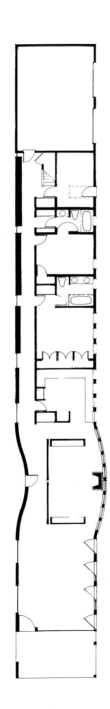
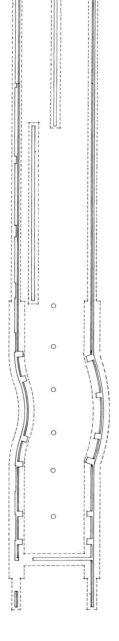

House in Surry

Surry, Maine

Landscape, geometry, and light interact to define this seaside dwelling. The program was for a retirement home and studio of a couple with a large extended family who would all come to visit during the summer. The owners have a lifetime of belongings, but a desire for uncluttered spaces and room to display their art. Hence, the open plan needed to be served by extensive storage space contained in a series of pods or "saddlebags" clipped onto the inland side of the house. The resultant principal living space, free of support services or structure, is a lofty room, 58 feet long, terminating in a massive chimney wall of cut local granite.

The site is a meadow with few trees, a broad pebble beach, and spectacular views of Blue Hill Bay and Mt. Desert Island. As this is a flood-plain area, regulation required the house to be built up off the ground with concrete piers to support the floor. These piers, extended up to eave height, carry the roof as well and establish an order of paired columns that bends and shifts to accommodate the landscape. To the columns are clipped steel beams and rafters, creating a continuous pavilion that floats above the ground. Within this ordered structure, storage elements, enclosed sleeping areas, folding decks, kitchen, and baths are inserted as free-standing objects wrapped or interposed with glass.

The open site is suffused with intense, un-shaded light, magnified further by reflection from the water scarcely 25 yards away. The light surrounds each component of the architecture, articulating the parts, dissolving the structural fabric, and creating an elusive, palpitant, mirage-like form.

Above: The end elevation reveals the basic structure of the house repeated at each bay, every sixteen feet for the length of the building. A pair of columns rise from the ground to carry, first, paired steel beams at floor level, and then extend to eave height to bear a composite roof structure of steel angle rafters infilled with wood panels.

Opposite Page: At the minimum allowed distance from the ocean, the house hinges at its mid-point to follow and embrace the curve of the shore. Located in a flood plain district, the house was required by regulation to be built above ground level.

Above: *Free from any load-bearing require-ments, the envelope of the house can be entirely glass. Expressed at each corner, glass meets glass in a minimalist transparent joint, sharply contrasting with the sturdy structural column outside it.*

Opposite Page: *At the moment where the building opens, the "hinge," a single column bears both pavilion roofs. The roofs nearly touch at this apex, clearly articulating the implied continuity of structure from one pavil-ion to the next.*

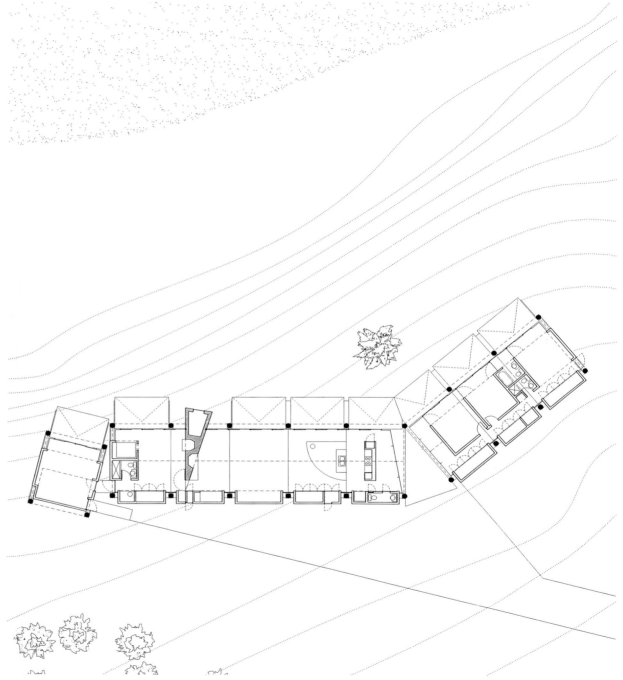

Right: Under the externally supported roofs, internal partitions, again free of any major structural requirement, are organized to enclose a consistent block of space down the center of each pavilion. Seen here, the end wall of that partitioned interior space appears as a free-standing plane within the enclosing glass envelope.

Top: *At the division of the two principal sections of the dwelling, the continuous space is sliced by mullion-less glass walls.*

Center: *Approaching the ocean side of the entrance penetration, the full breadth of the view is both revealed and reflected in the enclosing glass walls.*

Bottom: *Reflections and refractions of light, view, and the building itself appear to dissolve the structure and the enclosure, heightening the importance of the continuous sheltering roof.*

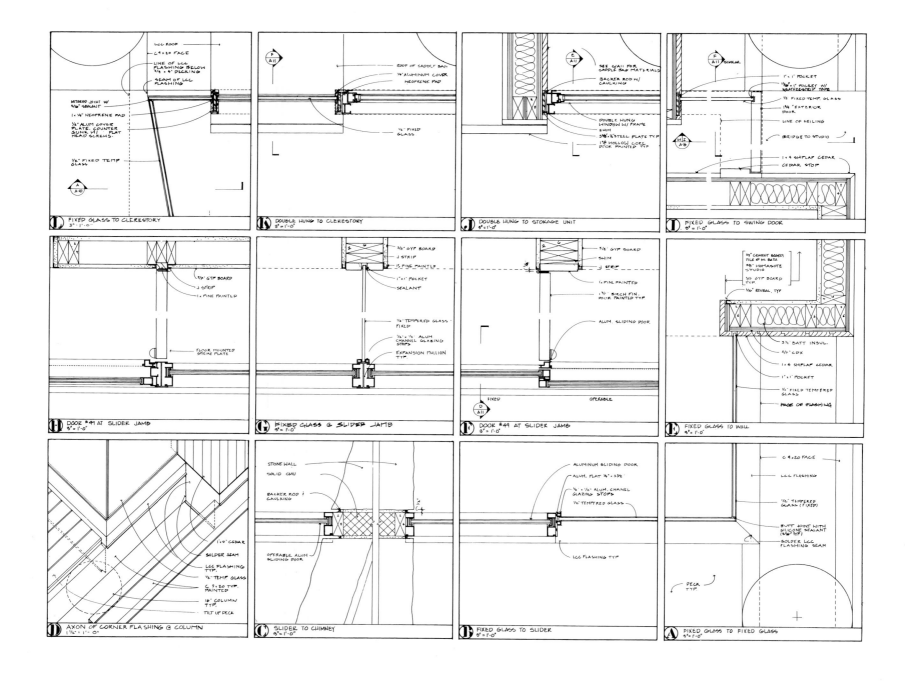

J FIXED GLASS TO CLERESTORY
3"=1'-0"

K DOUBLE HUNG TO CLERESTORY
3"=1'-0"

J DOUBLE HUNG TO STOKAGE UNIT
3"=1'-0"

I FIXED GLASS TO SWING DOOR
3"=1'-0"

H DOOR #41 AT SLIDER JAMB
3"=1'-0"

G FIXED GLASS @ SLIDER JAMB
3"=1'-0"

F DOOR #49 AT SLIDER JAMB
3"=1'-0"

E FIXED GLASS TO WALL
3"=1'-0"

D AXON OF CORNER FLASHING @ COLUMN
1½"=1'-0"

C SLIDER TO CHIMNEY
3"=1'-0"

B FIXED GLASS TO SLIDER
3"=1'-0"

A FIXED GLASS TO FIXED GLASS
3"=1'-0"

Right: *The public and private realms of the main house are divided by the granite chimney. On the near side is a great room encompassing living, dining, and kitchen. Beyond the chimney is the master bedroom and bath.*

Opposite Page: *Along the inland side of the entire house are a series of prefabricated modules, which contain storage, bathrooms, laundry facilities, pantry, and the like. A continuous ribbon of clerestory window runs above the modules, interspersed at each column with floor-to-ceiling operable windows.*

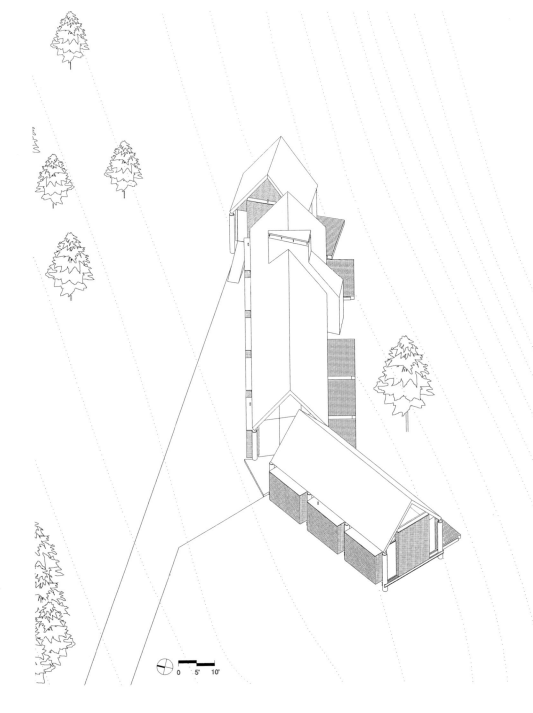

Selected Buildings
and Projects

House in Marion
Marion, Massachusetts

Consultants: Louis H. Conklin c/o
Stone and Webster (structural)
General Contractor: Houdelette Co.
Lot Size: 4 Acres
Building Size: 3800 sf
Date of Design: 1985-1987
Contruction Completed: 1987

House on Mount Desert Island
Mount Desert Island, Maine

Consultants: Zaldastani Associates, Inc.
(structural); Panitsas Associates, Inc.
(mechanical); General Contractor: John
Ruger Associates
Lot Size: 5 Acres
Building Size: 2,000 sf
Date of Design: 1991-1993
Contruction Completed: 1993

House at Seal Cove
Seal Cove, Maine

Consultants: Louis Conklin (structural)
General Contractor: Victor W. Mercer, Inc.
Lot Size: 1.5 Acres
Building Size: 1250 sf
Date of Design: 1982
Contruction Completed: 1983

House on Deer Isle
Deer Isle, Maine

Consultants: Zaldastani Associates,
Inc. (structural); Goldman Associates,
Inc. (mechanical); General Contractor:
Prin Allen and Sons
Lot Size: 50 Acres
Building Size: 2300 sf
Date of Design: 1984-1985
Contruction Completed: 1985

House at Cape Rosier
Cape Rosier, Maine

Lot Size: 5 Acres
Building Size: 4000 sf
Date of Design: 1989

House at Orcutt Harbor
Orcutt Harbor, Maine

Consultants: Zaldastani Associates, Inc.
(structural); Panitsas Associates, Inc.
(mechanical); General Contractor:
Phil Urban Fine Homes
Lot Size: 5.1 Acres
Building Size: 3700 sf
Date of Design: 1991-1993
Contruction Completed: 1993

House in Mattapoisett
Mattapoisett, Massachusetts

Consultants: Stone and Webster
(structural); Megatech Corperation
(mechanical)
General Contractor: Fisher and Rocha
Lot Size: 7 acres
Building Size: 3800 sf
Date of Design: 1984
Contruction Completed: 1985

House on Great Cranberry Island
Great Cranberry Island, Maine

Consultants: Zaldastani Associates
(structural); General Contractor:
Victor Mercer, Inc. and Michael
Westphal/Builder
Lot Size: 4 acres
Building Size: 3000 sf
Date of Design: 1985-1987
Contruction Completed: 1987

House on Potomac River
Washington, D.C.

Consultants: Lewis H. Conklin (struc-
tural); General Contractor: Peterson
and Collins, Inc.
Lot Size: 7100 sf
Building Size: 3200 sf
Date of Design: 1989-1992
Contruction Completed: 1992

House in Surry
Surry, Maine

Consultants: Zaldastani Associates,
Inc. (structural); Panitsas Associates,
Inc. (mechanical); General Contractor:
Phil Urban Fine Homes
Lot Size: 4 Acres
Building Size: 3200 sf
Date of Design: 1992-1993
Contruction Completed: 1995

with offices in Boston, Massachusetts. Within four years the firm had expande
its practice, opened branch offices in Maine and New York City, and was
engaged in projects throughout the United States. Since that time Peter Forbe
and Associates have become celebrated for their architecture of rigorously
simple forms, carefully sited in the landscape and meticulously detailed.

The firm was first recognized by the cover story in *Architectural Record* maga-
zine of December 1981, followed by Record House Awards in 1983, 1986, 1987
and 1989. In 1986 Peter Forbes and Associates received the National Honor
Award for a house designed on Deer Isle, Maine, only the third National Hono
Award ever given to a building in Maine and still the only such award given to
a house in Maine. With the extensive publication of this house throughout the
world architectural press and its subsequent receipt of six additional awards,
Peter Forbes and Associates became established as one of a very few firms who
primarily focus on residential architecture at the highest level of design. They
were further distinguished in an era of fleetingly transient fashions in design a
a firm committed to timeless architecture, neither trendy nor historicist, excel-
lently constructed of materials that would endure. For this work the firm has
received over thirty design awards and has been extensively published in peri-
odicals and professional journals in America, Europe, and Asia.

Throughout the history of the firm, Peter Forbes and Associates have been
selected to design a variety of building types, commercial, institutional, and
public as well as residential. The common denominator of these commissions
and the resulting buildings has been an imperative to evolve innovative solutions to design problems that have few, if any, precedents. Whether the program demanded an exploration of alternative materials to produce a toxin-fre
environment or the invention of low energy, low environmental-impact structures for the military, or an urban residential prototype that mitigated the
effects of dense urban settlement and noise—including the now ubiquitous
intrusion of aircraft sound— these were not conditions that could be resolved

demands, required an independence from reliance upon past solutions. Each necessitated intense analysis of program, client and site specifics, often resulting in the development of innovative materials, systems and fabrication techniques. Peter Forbes and Associates approach architecture without stylistic "baggage," achieving new solutions to complex problems from within the needs and desires of the client and the dictates of the site.

As important as their involvement is with technical innovation, Peter Forbes and Associates is equally engaged in re-examining the cultural parameters that underlie society's need for architecture. The basic tenet of their architecture is that to design is, in essence, to explain: the function, the role or the meaning of the designed object in its universe. Only through its relationship to the orders, ceremonies, and beliefs of a culture can technical innovation achieve meaning beyond the most immediate functional response. Only when design is in resonance with intrinsic human concerns, not superficial preconceptions, can it ascend from mere shelter to genuine architecture. This resonance is constantly changing; its determination, a constant search. That exploration is what the architecture of Peter Forbes and Associates is about.

Above: Peter Forbes

It is impossible to make good architecture without good clients. Peter Forbes and Associates have been particularly blessed with good clients for each of the houses featured here.

Daniel and Nancy Mahoney; Natalie Miller; David and Mardee Nordberg; Richard and Anne Silven; Michael Sinclair; Robert and Irene Sinclair; Gregg and Lisa Stone; Rodman and Susan Ward; Ned and Patty Wharton; Gary and Joyce Wenglowski.

Photographic Credits